The Big Day!
First Day of School

Nicola Barber

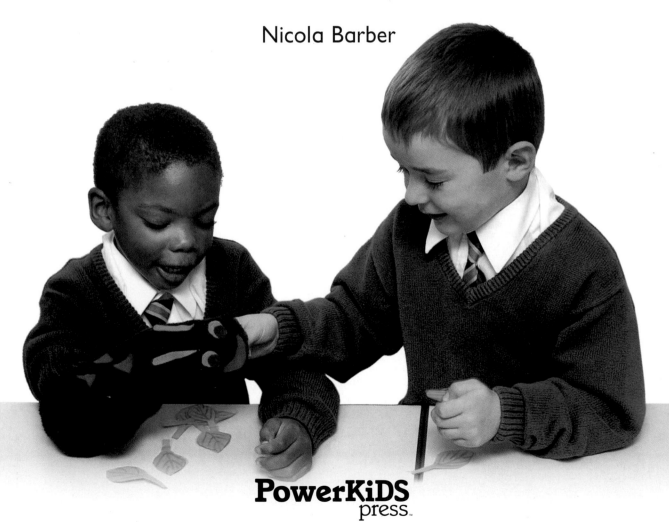

PowerKiDS
press.

New York

Published in 2009 by The Rosen Publishing Group Inc.
29 East 21st Street, New York, NY 10010

Copyright © 2009 Wayland/The Rosen Publishing Group, Inc.

First Edition

Editor: Camilla Lloyd
Designer: Elaine Wilkinson
Picture Researcher: Kathy Lockley

Library of Congress Cataloging-in-Publication Data

Barber, Nicola.
   First day of school / Nicola Barber. — 1st ed.
       p. cm. — (The big day!)
   Includes index.
   ISBN 978-1-4358-2839-1 (library binding)
   ISBN 978-1-4358-2895-7 (paperback)
   ISBN 978-1-4358-2899-5 (6-pack)
   1. First day of school—Juvenile literature. 2. Early childhood education—Juvenile literature.
   I. Title.
   LB1139.23.B37 2009
   372.12'44—dc22

                                              2008025816

Manufactured in China

Picture Acknowledgments: The author and publisher would like to thank the following for their
pictures to be reproduced in this publication: Cover photograph and 20: Adrian Sherratt/Alamy
Images; Angela Hampton/Bubbles Photolibrary: 10; Chris Fairclough: 14, 15; Gideon
mendel/Corbis: 13, 19; Janine Wiedel Photo Library/Alamy Images: 5; Jennie Hart/Alamy Images:
21; Jennie Woodcock/Bubbles Photolibrary: 7; Matt Henry Gunther/Taxi/Getty Images: 9; Olaf
Doering/Alamy Images: 6; Ronnie Kaufman/Corbis: 12, 24; Sally & Richard Greenhill/Alamy
Images: 1, 18; Steve Skjold/Alamy Images: 11; Teegan Mason: 17; Wayland Archive: 16;
www.shoutpictures.com: 8.

Contents

Starting school

Soon it will be the big day—your first day at school.

What will school be like?

You have probably visited your new school and met your new teacher. Have you talked to your brother or sister about school?

4

Your Mom or Dad might read you some stories about going to school.

Getting ready

What will you wear at your new school?
In some schools, children wear their normal,
everyday clothes.

In other schools, children wear special clothes,
called a uniform. Your Mom or Dad will take
you to buy the clothes you need for school.

You will need a book bag to carry your
books and work. You might need to choose
a lunchbox, too.

Going to school

How will you get to school?
If you live close by, you might be able
to walk, or go on your bike.

If you live farther away, your Mom or Dad may take you in the car. Or you might go on the school bus or by train.

Saying goodbye

When you get to school, your teacher will be there to say hello.

You say goodbye to your parents. You might feel a bit sad, but you will see them again in the afternoon.

You can hang your coat and bag on a peg in the closet. Your teacher will show you where your classroom is.

In your classroom

There are all kinds of things
to do in your classroom.
You can draw and paint,
or make models.
You can play with
sand or water.

You can look at books, or practice writing. Sometimes you might go to a different room to work on the school computers.

Playtime

Playtime is fun!
If the weather is nice, you can go outside.

Some schools have equipment for climbing, swinging, and sliding. You can play games in the playground, too.

If you are feeling a little bit lonely or sad,
you can sit on the playground bench and
ask some friends to sit with you.

Lunchtime

It's lunchtime and you are hungry. Your teacher will take you to the school dining room, or to the hall that is used for lunch.

The lunchtime assistants will help you to choose your lunch. There's dessert, too!

You might pack your own lunch at home in a lunchbox and bring that to school.

 # Making friends

You might already know some of the
children in your class. You will soon
start to make new friends, too.

At playtime, you can play games with
your friends.

Going home

When it is time to go home, everyone helps to tidy up the classroom. Then your teacher might read a story, or you might sing some songs.

You take your bag and coat from your peg. Your teacher says goodbye and makes sure there is someone to meet you and to take you home safely.

How was your first day?

School words

If you are writing about starting school, these are some of the words you might need to use.

Classroom

Lunchbox

Closet

Peg

Equipment

Playtime

Playground

Story

Going home

Teacher

Lunch

Uniform

Further information

Books

Billy and the Big New School
by Laurence Anholt (Albert Whitman and Company, 2002)

Do I Have to Go to School?: A First Look at Starting School
by Pat Thomas (Barron's Educational, 2006)

Going to School (Usborne First Experiences)
by Anne Civardi (Usborne Books, 2005)

I Am Too Absolutely Small for School
by Lauren Child (Candlewick, 2005)

Starting School
by Franzeska Ewart (Parragon Publishing, 2006)

Web Sites

Due to the changing nature of Internet links, PowerKids Press has developed an online list of Web sites related to the subject of this book. This site is updated regularly. Please use this link to access this list:
www.powerkidslinks.com/bd/school

Index